PEACE IN PIECES

PEACE IN PIECES

A Memoir Told Through Poetry

PEGGY BELLES

Peace in Pieces, A Memoir Told Through Poetry. Copyright 2017 Peggy Belles

All rights reserved. No part of this book may be used or reproduced by any means, graphic, electronic, or mechanical, including photocopying, recording, taping or by any information storage retrieval system without the written permission of the author except in the case of brief quotations embodied in critical articles, reviews and certain other noncommercial uses permitted by copyright law. For permission requests or information contact Peggy Belles at peggybelles@peggybelles.com or visit Peggy Belles Transformational Consulting at peggybelles.com

ISBN-13: 9780692936566

ISBN-10: 0692936564

Library of Congress Control Number: 2017912836
Peggy Belles, Tuckahoe, NY

Printed in the United States of America

Young author at work. Peggy, age 4.

CONTENTS

Dedication · xi
Foreword · xv
Introduction · xvii

Chapter 1   Once Upon A Time · 1
Home 3
What's In a Name 5
The Master Glass Sniffer 7
Brown Basin 8
Red, White, and Blue 9
Red Ocean 10

Chapter 2   The Journey · 13
The Edge of Pain 17
Uninvited 18
One Sixteenth 21
The Quilt 23
A Great Month For Dying 25
My Will Be Done 26
Sacrifice 28
Home Repairs 29
Shame 30
This Time 31
I Am 32
Taking Stock 35

Chapter 3	The Business of Living	39
	The Trouble With Gray	41
	Take Off	42
	I Want To Love you, But I Don't	43
	Let's Pretend	44
	Gone	45
	Unreported Crime	47
	I Don't Understand	49
	Under Cover	50
	Reality Check	51
Chapter 4	Goodbyes Are Hard	53
	A Shore In Montauk	55
	Promises Kept	56
	Her Words	57
	Bloody Mary	58
Chapter 5	The Awakening	61
	At The Seams	65
	Faces	66
	Ego	67
	Onion	68
	Singular	69
	Mom, I Only Met You Today	70
	Dementia Fixes Everything	72
	Blood	74
	Mulberry	75
	All Rise	76
	Acknowledgments	81
	About The Author	83

DEDICATION

This collection is dedicated, with all of my love and heart, to my family.
Danny, Alexa, Justin, Lauren, Daniel, Brandon, Jeannette, Tom, Dean and Adrian:
All that I offer is in honor of each one of you. Your love, support and encouragement is what makes it all happen, and makes it all matter. I love you!

For my mother, who I have come to know more intimately after her death, than ever in her life: My beautiful, selfless mother, for whom I would trade it all to spend just one more day with her; she impacted me more than she could have ever imagined and taught me more than she ever believed.
I miss and love you Mom.

For my sister Vivian who finally found peace: I love you.

And to Lucille, my sister by soul, who always believed in me:
This one is for you, with all of my love.

Peggy, age 13, with her sisters and brother on her Confirmation day.

FOREWORD

I remember my first meeting with Peggy. I was teaching "Beginning Memoir" and she entered the classroom with a huge, generous smile on her face and an enthusiasm that made me immediately take notice of her. She sat next to an older gentleman who had isolated himself from the others in the group, and within a few minutes they were chuckling together and seemed like old friends. After the first writing exercises, however, it soon became obvious, that, as she writes, "I am nothing like what I appear to be." Peggy's vibrancy and guileless openness belied a depth of character that had experienced trauma, shame, shattering betrayals, heart-pounding work experiences, personal and professional sacrifices, and a complex family life representing "a mélange of the world."

Over the years that I have known Peggy, I have had the privilege of witnessing, and benefitting from, her strength, wisdom, and spiritual depth. She is a person who radiates kindness because she *works* each day to cultivate understanding--of herself, and others. She has distilled her knowledge into training programs (the clinics in the hospital where I work greatly benefitted from one of these trainings) and individualized counseling sessions, with the goal of helping individuals and organizations achieve their full potential—despite and in spite of challenges and setbacks.

At the beginning of her career in law enforcement, Peggy took an oath to protect and serve. As you read this precious volume of poems, you will soon see that this professional duty has evolved into a life quest—not just to protect and serve the vulnerable "other," but to nurture and restore to health her own vulnerable self. This striving is not an easy feat for one who can see with clarity the underbelly of human nature, but rather than become hardened and embittered by life experiences, she has used her "grey Blackwing pencil" to make sense of her universe--all while never losing sight of the humor, love, coincidences, friendships and treasured moments that also enabled her to grow and heal. Through her honest reflections on life and love, pain and suffering, she reveals to us the unshakeable power of compassion—for self and for others. Let her words comfort and inspire you as she takes you, piece by piece, on the universal human journey of self-discovery.

Sarajane Brittis, Ph.D.
August 2017

INTRODUCTION

Poems come to life when I sleep; they wake me up at night begging to be written. They each tell a story, and together this collection of poetry is my memoir.

A self proclaimed writer since the age of four, I learned early on that placing pencil to paper allowed me to make sense of the world and the people in it. I have always been in love with words, and writing about life has sustained me. Experiences that I could not understand, and those that could not be voiced, were written. We all have an exterior, and the preferred angle for a photo. We also have the interior, the side that is hidden from the lens. I'm fascinated by the unseen. The polished and seemingly unscathed version of ourselves is what the world usually gets to see, yet it is vulnerability that draws me in. I find that there is far more courage in vulnerability and what lies beyond the resume, and that is what my poems seek to explore and reveal.

When speaking to groups, I usually introduce myself with one of my poems, as it is my way to connect with people on a heart level. This collection runs the gamut from childhood, identity, domestic violence, alcoholism, motherhood, racism, career, love, betrayal, death, hope, forgiveness and peace. The themes are universal, as I believe we are all a reflection of one another.

I offer these poems to you, my reader and kindred seeker of self, a divine agreement between us. I invite you in, and to read each word and line until you feel them, until you are there, or wherever it is that they may lead you to go. My hope is that this collection will leave you inspired to be exactly who you are.

August 2, 1973

Vivian, Peggy, and Bonnie
33 Terrace Place

CHAPTER 1
ONCE UPON A TIME

Sometimes you have to go back to the beginning of the story, so that you will understand the rest.

HOME

The hole,
searing through her soul.
My soul.
emptiness,
a black cloak of shame,
Familiar.
A vestment comfortably worn over
      every *thing*.

Now,
I stand before the mirror, fasten each button
donning a white shirt, dressed with gold bars,
a shining badge in place, proud
      in tact.

Then,
darkness eclipsing light,
caverns for hiding
underneath the bed
long ago
in the closet, covering my ears
      safe.
Sparkling remnants of tinsel,
a few ornaments still alive,
Gold and Red shattered.

In my father's drunken rage,
a sea of pennies hurled
falling from the sky

like unexpected rain showers,
landing on grass green carpet,
    scattered.
Our Christmas tree
donning its decorations,
thrown from the porch, to the snow blanketed lawn below,
a launched missile.
War, Battlefield, Casualties,
    Home.

WHAT'S IN A NAME

Margaret Dorothea Nolan,
a nightmare of a name for a Catholic school girl.
Twenty-one letters was the real problem,
though my parents called me Peggy since the day I was born.
Everyone did, except the nuns
and others who really didn't know me.

The unanswered question remains,
why would my parents give a name
that they never intended to use?

My two sisters fared far better in the name game,
one sister, Vivian June,
the other, Bonnie Mae,
and me,
the twenty-one lettered Margaret Dorothea.
I wished for a cute name like Maggie or Meg,
but definitely not Peg.
My brother's letter tally
came in at twenty, yet he
seemed to make the best of it.

Once married, I traded half
of my name for a new one.
Then came changing titles
and other letters
affixed to define,
more boxes to check.

Now, I wear names like garments,
choosing some, often changing,
shedding and releasing others.

I stand free,
staring each one in the eye,
believing I no longer have to slip them on anymore.

I am free at last.

THE MASTER GLASS SNIFFER

"Marc, why do I get a knot in my stomach when I open the front door?"
His blue eyes fixed on me, "Go back and remember."
So that was it? It was about remembering? Why didn't I think of that?
Maybe I had thought of it,
but preferred forgetting.

Every day, the Catholic school uniform was the same,
navy plaid skirt, knee high blue socks, and Famolare shoes to match.
We all *looked* the same.

The walk from the bus stop to 33 Terrace Place
was short by measure of distance,
and long in measure of apprehension.
I was at my door by 3pm,
      my *front* door.

The sound of loud music was a foreboding,
a warning to seek out a sleepover
somewhere, *anywhere*.
In these cases, there was no need
to find a glass to sniff for proof.

An early apprenticeship,
valuable on the job training
in pupil watching and voice pitch,
with a Master's degree in the art of glass sniffing.

BROWN BASIN

The chocolate brown plastic basin sat
to the left side in my Nanny's kitchen sink,
filled to the brim with warm sudsy, soapy water.

Dishwashing was not always a mundane activity,
especially forty years ago,
standing on her kitchen chair
so I could reach
and help to wash and dry the dinner dishes,
an important job for my seven year old self,
where a night's work yielded one dollar.

I loved to swish my hands around in the water filled basin,
deliberately moving the dishrag over and under the plates,
inside and outside of the glasses,
rinsing and re-rinsing
to be sure they wouldn't taste like the bright green Palmolive dish soap,
      washing them clean.

Sometimes my sisters had a station too.
Vivian washed, I dried, and Bonnie put them away.
This ritual of normal chores created a longed-for belonging.

The normal part,
that's what stands out.
We were normal, like other families,
even if it was only when we washed dishes.

RED, WHITE, AND BLUE

And of my own hand,
a thin white scar
barely visible, atop a deep blue vein.
Its brutal truth contained.
Once a gushing red river.

RED OCEAN

That July day was sweltering, 92 degrees at 8am.
Rushing to ready for the party,
my arms pushed and swung
the back door open,
thrusting them through
the plate glass window.
The sight of the bright red blood transported me
right back to fifteen.
The day I first drew blood, I cannot remember,
sitting on my bathroom sink,
a beautiful robins egg blue,
when the sharp blade
found just the right angle,

like a pot of water coming to a boil,
thrashing and hitting the confines.
"Help me!" I screamed, *inside*.
Nobody heard, nobody came.

The waves crashed,
droplets of blood falling,
in pools onto the porcelain blue-

red and blue, a striking contrast.

Filled to the brim with desperation,
I couldn't stop it
the red kept coming
covering the blue,

I longed only to see the blue.
Tying it off slowed the rushing current,
    eventually it stopped.

That time it went too deep,
way deeper than ever before.

Now, like a monument to myself
the faded evidence sits quietly
on my wrist,
making no fuss at all.

And in *those* days, loneliness hugged me tightly,
like arms wrapped around my heart.
A veil of sadness,
like a gentle wind blowing
ever so softly,
not disruptive, always having manners,
on its best behavior.

And *these* days,
I still love the ocean,
beauty, mystery, power,
    quiet rage,
all hidden beneath the surface,

the outer and inner layers,
Above and Beneath.

CHAPTER 2

THE JOURNEY

Pain is a great teacher if we are ready to learn.

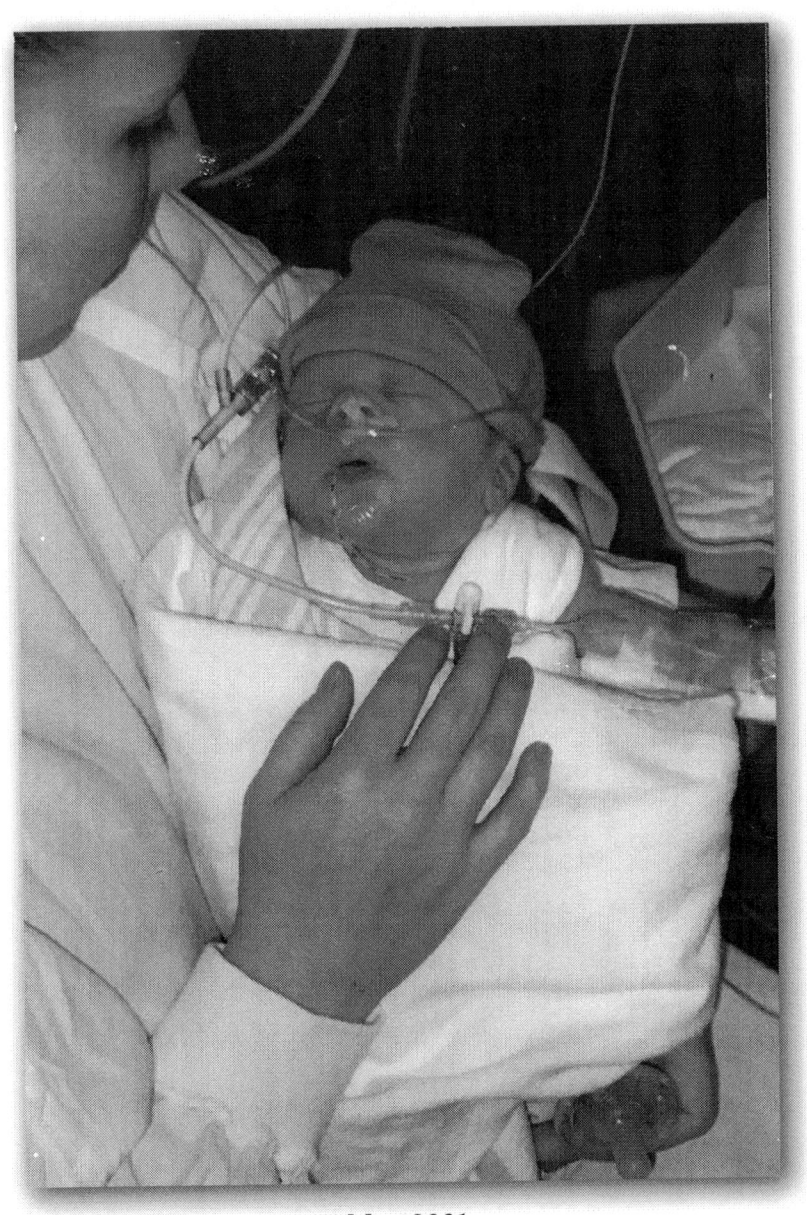

May, 2001
Miracles happen.

THE EDGE OF PAIN

would feel nice,
comforting.
It would be enough to stay at the edge,
like the serrated blade of a knife
so sharp to the touch before it tears through.
The potential to be immersed and swallowed
up, saturated in the throbbing,
screaming ripped-openness.
The edge of pain allows you to gaze upon it,
yet allows you to stay
just far enough away.
Stay with me
here.

UNINVITED

Death held my sister's hand
    walking *slowly* quietly in step,
Ten years longer than the sentence delivered
by her doctor,
    40 birthdays, 3 months, 7 days.

    Camera lights flashing, glossy prints capturing
        innocence.
    Platinum pin straight tresses to blonde bouncing curls
    Raw beauty, ocean blue eyes
    Your scent; powder, Jean Nate, baby oil, fresh.

        Now dollars paid,
        Exchanged, Purchasing every ounce
        of self worth.
        Dark staircases soaked in urine,
        buildings crumbling
        Harlem and *company;* far from their heyday.
        Untold stories of hard living on every step, in every line, every vein
            Runways to alleyways.

        Me, wearing too big blue platform high heeled shoes
        pretending I was You,
        waiting, waiting, *always* waiting for you
        hot rollers, makeup waiting too.
        My reflection in your vanity mirror; lights
            Disco, Nighttime, Daylight.

The day would arrive unannounced
when finally you were home
plastic red frosted glass in hand
sweet, sugary lemon iced tea
      Full, Loaded like a syringe.

      Watching afternoon soap operas
      with you while you nodded
      off in your green flowered chair
      Maybe dreaming now free
      as you sleep
      not owned by the street
      Home. Safe.

A mother's dream of a silver spoon life
      Sold.
Spoons *cooking*
Needles aching to plunge
Which held the uninvited One?

      Blue veins vanishing
      longing for that place where
      all feeling dissolves
      floating but drowning
      glistening drops of brown heaven mixed with hell, Delivered.

      The invader, the virus
           the uninvited one taking you away.

      The day my son came into this world
      you made one more stop before goodbye,

Both of you living on borrowed breath
    in separate spaces where life and death
hold hands.

And in the end
a skeleton ravaged,
infection stealing away with your sight
in one leaving
a single beautiful blue eye.

    I still share your dying last words
    living in ears needing to hear
        your pain
        another tortured soul's deliverance.

    My boy made it
    defying odds

        Perhaps you traded your life for his?

        I remember how your haunting
            eyes always slept
            half open.
        I'm sure you know,
            he sleeps like you.

ONE SIXTEENTH

Do not be fooled by the box
for it does not matter which is checked,
your mark already decided
my son and daughter.
One drop

children, not white
nor black
Both and Neither
solely none.

Brown eyes, *good* hair
society cast its vote
deciding
by shade which is passing,
but really *I* know
even one drop
assures there is no pass,
just degrees of acceptance.
One drop

Light or dark
house or field negro,
their lot in life decided by their masters.
Jim Crow segregation, Racial Integrity Law,
illusions of *passing*
by measures of one sixteenth.
history lived not so long ago.
One drop

Oh no longer segregated
no doubt separated
minds stay
unchanged.
Today, words
carefully crafted and chosen,
right and fair.
One drop

Black,
a description *still* spoken in hushed tones.
Mother's skin,
your Mother's skin,
the hue of your oppressors.
My skin, Our skin.

THE QUILT

Each square represents snapshots of your life
capturing time within each border.
Touch each one, the places where beads of sweat collected
mixed with both tears of joy and sadness.
All now dry, invisible to the eye.

The soaked fabric enshrining your heart absorbing it all.
Hear the cheers, hear the silence.
See the smiles and the fans. See the empty bleachers
and hours of shots, ball after ball.
Remember what you won and what you lost, both having nothing to do with
the game.

As you sit and read books to your son tell him stories
of three point jump shots, or the foul line where you stood
while everyone watched,
hoping that you would make it, or praying that you would miss.

Teach him about victory, teach him of defeat.
Don't leave out defeat.

The moments of glory sit beside the painful ones,
stitched together whole and intact,
woven as one tapestry spanning years,
just like life.

Tell him to ask about the blank space
in between the squares, where it seems to be just
border holding the more important things,

explain that the borders *are* the important things.
The space where nothing appears to be is exactly where everything is.

He will weave his own squares of time.
Maybe he too will play basketball, and maybe he won't,
but he will dream his own dreams.

In the center, sits the Nolan name,
emblazoned on the shirt that held my dreams in 1994,
the year that you were born.
I wore it in the police academy, as I tried to build a life.

Now it finds its home representing a legacy of love, to cover your family.
Keep the roots strong. Let the quilt remind you
that we will always be branches of the same tree.
I love you all with my whole heart,

Mom

A GREAT MONTH FOR DYING

My family loves to die in May
      they all do it.
I certainly will do it too.
May,
a great month for dying,
beautiful flowers bloom for funerals.
Mom, Nanny, Great Grandma
Texas cousins too.

One sister's middle name is Mae
      and that just might save her.
My oldest sister Vivian chose to die in June,
perhaps as it matched her middle name.

Soft, coffee colored earth, light
painless to shovel,
and dig graves.

May,
alive with new life,
warm air, sweet scents.
Yes indeed, a great month
for dying!

MY WILL BE DONE

I could not cremate my mother,
That was *her* wish.

My spontaneous decision not
to send her into flames
can never be changed.

She sleeps in a grave
she never wanted, yet
has no choice but to reside.

Could ignorance of youth suffice
as the excuse to deny my mother
her final resting place?

Although my love and honor for her was undying,
my own selfish will
was the winner of the draw.

The roots of our tree.

SACRIFICE

No one heard the crack
      there was no goodbye,
they just went their separate ways
fractured and mangled.

I stared at the pieces set atop blackness.
My eyes only wanted to see the black,
not the jagged chasm
not the separateness.

When I stared long enough
listening close,
I heard them calling
out to each other,
longing for wholeness
dying to return.

The cut was deep
tearing, creating
an opening
to take away from the strong, intact one,
to strengthen the weak.

One had to give
      it could sacrifice
just this once.

HOME REPAIRS

Maybe fixing you
fixes me.
Maybe that's why the grip is always so tight
around your neck,
Choking off the choices for you,
     since I couldn't do that for myself.

Reliving my entire life now
from the other side of the fence,
     getting to see it all from both sides.

I don't want the fence.

Maybe neither of us ever *need*ed the fixing part,
     just the love.

SHAME

It stays in the closet
Banging against the door, thrashing
Its ugly black body hard,
It shakes.

I check to make sure it can't escape,
slimy tarantula fingers barely squeezing out from the space beneath the door,
Reaching to assault me again.
I see its demon yellow eyes.
It's quiet,
breathing and waiting,
Maybe sleeping.

Today it was laying heavy on top of me, groping
with its tentacles,
strangling me breathless with its appendages.
I swung,
hitting it hard.

I shot up in bed, to hear it moving
safe inside of the closet.

THIS TIME

How can I destroy my beautiful life,
this time?
Wind up and hurl it against the wall to see
how much It takes to shatter,
in hundreds of glistening, shiny pieces.

The familiar naturalness of broken,
a release from the wholeness of it all.

Come and help me smash it again,
I want to ask,
       but I don't.

I AM

Walking through the park
I see you
       alone.
Blonde hair
lying tucked away in a corner under the tree
       a white lotus flower adorns your towel

Why are you laying there?
At any moment he could attack,
Rape you while the birds sing and the sun shines looking
on buttercups and dandelions side by side
       like witnesses seeing all but will not tell.

Up until today, if asked what I did for a living,
I would say that I once was a cop.
That is not true,
I am one.
That will always be true
       not for what I did, but for what I cannot do.

I am watching
you are not worried
       sleeping, soaking in the sun
not afraid
not vulnerable
Prey.

I cannot see your face
from where I am sitting on the bench, a stone's throw away
     I stand watch
On guard, protecting

The cars go by
close, yet far enough away
     they won't hear your screams for help
They, in their mobile compartments
singing, talking
     not observing.

Why do you feel so safe? *I want to know.*
How do you close your eyes? *These things I cannot do.*
What is wrong with you? *No. What is wrong with me?*

The butterflies dance in pairs overhead,
You turn your face to the sun.

Mentally recording the details
I am noting all of the facts,
     for the report.
Southeast corner of the park. White female, 5'5, blonde shoulder length hair, wearing black shorts, white tee shirt, silver wrist watch on left hand, sunglasses, tan backpack.

I have to leave now.
I note the time 3:32PM, *last time seen*, and gather my things to leave.
I turn one last time I see you fill your backpack.
Toting your yoga mat in a bright orange bag, I watch you slip
into your black sandals.
I decide to stay until you leave.

You are happy and free as you walk away,
      at least that is how it appears.
I am nothing like what I appear to be.

TAKING STOCK

My grey Blackwing pencil. The eraser is barely there.

My mind that races. The engine starts every morning at 5am.

My four kids. All four think I have a favorite-each believes it's not them.

My four separate journals-my favorite has a yellow bird on the cover.

My pencil case collection-my favorite is a vintage red case from Japan.

My ninety eight pound Doberman named Bo. He suffers from anxiety, but he isn't on medication.

My lazy right eye. It wanders when I'm tired and I always hope that nobody notices.

My Michael Kors silver watch with diamonds. It doesn't work anymore, but I pretend it does. It was a gift from my kids and covers the scar on my left wrist.

My blue calendar. Every day I try to fit my life inside of the boxes.

My husband. We found out anniversary dates can change.

My Mattel green inchworm toy from when I was 4. It still works and my grandson rides it.

My house built in 1880. We have been repairing it for thirteen years. It still needs repairs.

My original 1940's Chambers stove. It's yellow and the realtor tried to steal it after I bought my house.

My memory of the best Bloody Mary. I shared it with my friend in Nantucket two months before she died. She loved Bloody Mary's too.

Christmas Cards
December 2006

CHAPTER 3

THE BUSINESS OF LIVING

There is nothing easy about the business of living, yet no effort will ever be wasted.

THE TROUBLE WITH GRAY

Why is it so difficult to manage relationships?
And their shades of gray?

Easier to manage the tour of cops
Turning out with forty-five rounds,
Plus one in the chamber.

Procedural details,
Black or white.

Up on target,
Staring at life through the front sight, eye on the white dot, equal
light on either side, invisible face
            Center mass.
This time not up on a silhouette paper target,
The steel gray barrel carrying the round capable
of delivering death.

When I reach for the thumb break,
It's black and white.
Snap, open and draw,
The final decision made.
I can. I will.
It is my duty.

And so I guess,
that's the trouble with gray.

TAKE OFF

The oval shaped
peep window informed
my contained world.

I caught a glimpse of the tarmac
blanketed in white
below an endless steel
gray sky.

Take off always makes me feel important
sitting in my purchased seat
I have somewhere to go,
jitters in my stomach
excitement, vulnerability, mortality.

A delicate fine line hanging
in the balance.
Soaring, soaring higher
plummet, plunge
into frigid deep water.

I WANT TO LOVE YOU, BUT I DON'T

Your darkness was blinding,
Not like sunlight
in your eyes that makes it hard
to see.
A pitch black drape
covering my eyes
my voice, my heart.

I couldn't see
couldn't feel
anything but heaviness
weight, hate.

No I do not hate
anybody,
but I do hate you.

I finally faced
you head on,
now my equal
no longer my oppressor.

I'm standing in the light
     I can see.
Keep your darkness,
you can't keep me.

LET'S PRETEND

I liked it better when you pretended to love me,
I'm like all of the others now,
the ones you always talked about.
Now the absence of your texts
that once annoyed me,
I miss

or maybe I don't.

Seeing your name appearing on the screen
to remind me that we have to keep pretending,
I didn't want you to call me,
I didn't want you not to call.

I always wondered where the edges of your caring lay
every day inching closer,
fading friends falling into memory.

I wanted to give up,
make you sorry I did,

and it's the hurt of knowing that you gave up first,
I finally found the edge.

GONE

I heard the crunch, then the last gasp of breath
leave a then lifeless body.
I tried with so many,
to save them all
somehow to return them to life.

I walked along the train tracks,
picked up remnants of the brain
once inside of a seventeen year old boy's skull.

I held the hand of a four year old
Scraggly haired, red head
little girl in a yellow sundress,
no underwear beneath.
She told stories I wish she never lived
and those I wish I never heard.

I wrote the statement of a black and blue bride,
her words only understood through a translator.
Purchased for a price,
paid with promises of living the American dream.

Uncried tears
so heavy
but I waited.

Words inside of a heart shaped shell,
ready to give them away,
for someone to help me
carry the weight.

Clinging to the lines,
Hanging
on until the pencil releases them to paper.

I pour them onto the pages
as more wait their turn.
I grieve for the words that have left me,
It's all gone.

UNREPORTED CRIME

She came home
took off her coat and hung
it on the brass hook in the hallway,

and carefully pulled each arrow out
from her chest and back.
They hurt coming out,
some were in deep,
that's the thing about arrows
you *expect* carnage from knives,
not arrows.

It's easier to leave them in place
but she decided
they would be too noticeable,
especially the one that ripped
clean through her white shirt
impaling her heart.
There was no gurgling or bubbles of blood,
evidence easy to hide.

She found her spot
exactly one pillow away
from center on the couch

steam rose from her cup of chamomile tea,

and for the length of a sigh,
she didn't notice
the frayed, electrified wires running
through her body.

Just another day at work.

I DON'T UNDERSTAND

What did he mean by that?
Actually, I didn't have to ask,
his meaning deafening and unmistakable,

I stared at his back,
waiting for him to turn around
to soften the edge of his words,
as they tore me to shreds.

Standing there, bleeding out,
a gaping wound,
slashed, but not mortally wounded, *yet*.

"Okay," I said,
turned and walked out
holding my ripped, scoured flesh,
pushing it back,

holding the pieces together.

UNDER COVER

The bubbles, feverishly dancing,
jumping, bouncing,
crashing, thrashing,
to a boil-
the combustion,
behind her smile.

They stand too close,
    not bravely,
just oblivious.

She forces the softness of her face,
the timbre of her voice,
while hiding a burning urge
to ferociously attack.

"It's no problem," she says,
with fangs under lips.

REALITY CHECK

The world is
scrolling down,
swiping left and right.
What makes us press, or not?
Like and love,
easy *here*.

Things aren't so obvious,
In *real* life.
Did we misinterpret
the true intention?

Online, we know
if the numbers rise or not,
who are friends are, and who loves us today.
If we need to know,
we can log on to see who cares.

Lucille and Peggy
The Best Bloody Mary
August 2016

CHAPTER 4

GOODBYES ARE HARD

Until we meet again...

A SHORE IN MONTAUK

I will see you every morning when the sun rises,
You will be the beam of light that opens my eyes.

I will feel your touch
when the sun warms my skin,
or when the rain falls.

I will hear your laugh
with each wave
that crashes to shore
your heartbeat as it pulls
each one back out to sea.

I will feel your breath
when the wind blows,
and your love in my soul,
for we were always one
anyway.

PROMISES KEPT

Matching bathing suits
one purple, one pink,
Both with white hearts.
Sharing secrets and scars,
Bound together, friends for life,

but now death is waiting
for you to arrive.
Not knowing how many breaths you hold,
I take your hand and your fear.
Before the last, I whisper in your ear
I will bury all that scared you,
and your dreams I will carry.

HER WORDS

I do hear you
asking so many times,
it's just hard to understand
all of the words at once.

They float in my head
trying to land,
to sink in.

I am trying so hard,

I hear you say, "I love you so much,"
I come to the edge of my ears where the words flow
in along with the morphine waves,
I keep swimming to the top after every one.

I'm holding my head just above the water, reaching out
my right hand for yours,
      They keep reaching for me too

This next one will take me.

BLOODY MARY

I saved a seat for you today
ordered one of our favorites,
a Bloody Mary just like
the one that we savored in Nantucket.
I toasted again
just like we planned,
only you weren't sitting across from me today.
I toasted anyway,

to your life, to your fierce courage,
to your indomitable spirit.
I celebrated our sisterhood
that we held onto for decades.

My smile has faded
but I keep at it,
I must.

And now as I sit
for the first time,
in quite a long time
words will not find voice.
I feel them somewhere deep,
back between that space
in the base of my throat.
They stay
reticent,
a quiet discontent,
swimming laps just below

the surface.
I don't know exactly
what the words would be
only that I will keep them,
I will hold onto thoughts of what they would tell.

I want to share them with you
and realize that I still could,
though they will hang in the air
dissolving into an empty,
loud silence.

I decide to hold on
to them,
and to possibilities.

CHAPTER 5

THE AWAKENING

"If a thousand suns were to have risen in the sky at once,
such brilliance as this might resemble the brilliance of the Supreme self."

-Bhagavad Gita

My Mother
Vivian June Nolan

AT THE SEAMS

When I'm holding up
the whole world on my shoulders,
my arms extended,
I can feel where I'm glued
back together.
Look closely and see the cracks in the creases,
once a dangling arm, now shored up,
stronger than before.

We show up dressed,
not hiding.
I see the faint jagged crack at your hairline,
and smile knowingly.
We look good,

there is something beautiful about put-back-together things,
no need to wonder how it feels to break.

I used to make sure
it wouldn't be noticed,
and now that place,
resilient and exposed,
I know it's the first I want you to see.

FACES

Six faces, only five I can see,
seated around the conference table,
talking about you,
and the naughty words that you say.
I wish you were here,
so they could see your hazel, green eyes,

But you are only four, and at nursery school,
because its Thursday, and you go to school,
like all of the other children.

I silently hope that you earn a sticker today,
the ones they give to you when you use kind words,

But it's really not the kind words they count,
    only the curses.

As we answer their questions, they fill in their blanks,
looking down to write, analyze, *judge*
the words you use, *fucker*.

There is one more word that instantly makes everyone uncomfortable,
and we are holding that one for you.

I wait until the end of the meeting,
and decide to drop the bomb,
    and watch their faces search for an appropriate response.

EGO

How far have you really traveled on the path you teach?
In the first round, you were overtaken,

she came for your blind spot

in an unconscious reflex,
you felt the tremor,

It was back. It slammed its chains,
and screamed to be released,
wrestling to break free.
No, no, no, never.
At all costs it *must* always stay chained.

Equanimity was as far away from you as the sun.
Ego, you are such a coward.
Take the punch, let it land
right upon your cheek.

Don't you know?
You can always get out of the ring,
alas, you were so foolish to enter.

ONION

Peeling the onion,

layer by layer,
shedding, each
paper thin sheath.
One by One
They go.

Getting to what can be used
tears come, it emanates,
filling, overpowering, *arriving*.

Power beneath.
A deliberate excavation,
degrees of separation are gone,
They played their part.

Bare and exposed
Your presence need not be announced,
      It cannot be ignored

SINGULAR

Contained,
the lid closed
off from the world surrounding it.
Solitude and singular,
the obvious of being only one.
The beauty of this circumstance rarely realized.
One lone, powerful word that wants to,
and can stand alone.
Apart in a belonging world,
a becoming world,
an absorbing of things, people and identities world.
Spending a lifetime forging,
pressure forcing to add,
only to subtract away later.
The separateness,
the seduction of this state of being,

the value of one.

MOM, I ONLY MET YOU TODAY

Desperate, caustic
battery acid guilt
eroded my insides on this breezy languid summer night.
I loved you before
I understood what love was,
though,
minus due compassion and understanding.

You loved me before you knew me,
completely.

I sorted through your papers today,
read your words,
written in black indelible ink,
the page wet with my tears
of longing.

I cried for the last twenty four years
because I missed you.
Tonight I cried *for* you,
      wanting to cry *with* you.

I'm now just four years younger than you
when you left this place,
      and it's only today that I met you.

I want to hug you,
tell you that you are guilty of nothing.
Is it possible to bleed and heal at the same time?

That happened.

DEMENTIA FIXES EVERYTHING

One day my father decided
not to bathe anymore,
perhaps he no longer saw a need,
to pretend.
The dirt was familiar, the same as the blue shirt,
matching his eyes, that he preferred
not to change.
His habits die hard.

Last month, the doctor diagnosed him with dementia,
now I readily offer that to fix everything,
though we really didn't need the diagnosis.

He goes to daycare,
plays games that are on the schedule,
like brain teasers at noon.
During registration at the Veteran's Hospital
the receptionist asked him for his mother's name,

now that was a brain teaser.

But he still loves to sing,
and the important things he remembers,
like Dick Haymes,
and every note and word of those songs,

and those things he can remember,
those things he *wants* to remember.
Single focus of a lost mind.

And so it seems, we have switched places,

I hope I do a good job.

BLOOD

The world runs through your veins,
I was there that night,
but don't remember what captivated
Both of you, father and son,
drawing your eyes to look,
and affix on the same.
Though you both did not see
the same thing
with your own eyes,
nor understand it,
in the same way.

As it was with us son,

the blood through his veins,
even more complex than yours.
A mélange of the world,
countries and continents travel
limb to limb.
Arendal and Africa,
County Carlow and Ponce.

MULBERRY

You fell at your ripest,
juiciest, when all had filled you,
flesh tearing at the seams.

Prime pick, sweet, luscious
      Full-bodied.
You grace the ground now
Purple,
You let go.

But you know what,
You are still the juiciest
most realized one,
the one that let go
of the branches, and the tree.

ALL RISE

Something drew me
to the nature garden today,
I walked two miles to come
and sit to find
a tangible quiet to take away
and bring home.

I stood before
the butter yellow daffodils,
They weren't preening
not trying to be adored,
or remembered.
They stood
Faces to the sun,
ignoring my stare
rooted and stretching
their necks long
looking to the place that sustains life.

As hard as I tried to encapsulate them,
their hue through my lens,
to take them home
I noticed the way
They continued to stand before me
not caring if I was impressed.

They weren't for the taking.

Daffodils stand,
without apology.

Montauk, New York
2015

The End
Is always another beginning...

ACKNOWLEDGMENTS

By its proper definition, the word acknowledgment means the action of expressing gratitude or appreciation for something. It is an impossible undertaking to adequately express the immeasurable gratitude that I have to so many people who contributed to this collection, and to my life. Some have painstakingly listened and helped with never ending edits, some have inspired poems, and some have ultimately inspired my growth. I know that due to space, I would never be able to list each person that has left their mark on my life, but it is true that every person who has crossed my path has certainly imprinted something upon me. I am blessed to be surrounded by deep rooted friendships, and those people know how dear they are to me.

I thank God for every day that I get another chance to open my eyes, and for another chance to dream.

To my family, always first and foremost, you each hold a piece of my heart. You are the reason for everything, and I will never take that for granted. Thank you for your true love and support. I love you!

Danny, thank you for your unconditional and unapologetic love. There isn't enough space to capture our journey, but we needed every step. This would never be possible without you. I offer to you my whole heart.

Alexa, Justin, Daniel, Brandon, Lauren, Dean, Adrian, Jeannette and Tom: This entire collection represents us as a whole. We are a family with deep roots, love and unbreakable bonds.

Lucille, I love you. Thank you for always loving and believing in me. This is for you. Until we meet again. And with all of my love for Julia D, all of the promises will be kept.

My eternal love for my Mom, Dad, Vivian, Bonnie, Billy, Auntie Viv, Nanny, Grandpa, Grandma, Shelley, Billy and Robin: Thank you for the profound impact that each of you have made in my life.

For the Coliskey family with love and gratitude: Thank you for summers, memories of mountains and bonfires and for helping me to cultivate a lifetime love of nature.

My deepest love, appreciation, and gratitude for my lifelines: Flo Palma, Maria Greco, and Caroline Cimons.

For their friendship and support, my love goes to Nicki Cacciola, Andrew Zirolnik, Valarie Sydnor, Charlene Lambrecht, Bev Lewis, and Dee Pinto.

Jill Ganassi, thank you for your wisdom and for being able to do what nobody else could ever do for me. I have so much respect and love for you.

My deepest appreciation to Joshua Rosenthal, the Institute for Integrative Nutrition, the IIN Book Launch Group, and the team at CreateSpace. I am so honored and thankful to have had the training and support to make this a reality. I am especially grateful for my accountability partners: Katy Weber, Frederica Winley-Tokponwey, and Julie Diaz!

Sarajane Brittis, thank you for your support from the day we met. I am so grateful for your guidance, insight, expertise, genuine friendship and love. Your beautiful words touched my soul.

Jayne Jenner, I am so grateful for your support, love, friendship and honest, keen eye. Thank you for the never ending encouragement and hours spent going over words and sentences.

Arlen Gargagliano, thank you for so clearly seeing the title to this collection. What a gift! I am so grateful for your support, friendship and love.

Adrienne Abromowitz, thank you for seeing my passion for poetry and always telling me to trust myself. Thank you for your insight, friendship, and love.

Chief John Costanzo, thank you for so many years of mentorship, friendship, amazing opportunities, and for believing in me.

Love to all of my colleagues and friends, retired and active, from the Tuckahoe Police Department.

My respect and love for my FBI National Academy brothers and sisters from #254, and my colleagues and friends in the New York State/Canada Chapter.

To my Hudson Writers Group, many thanks to all of you for listening and encouraging me.

Tania Moore and my Stories Alive community, Stan Martin, Susan Van Sciver, Dorothy Maillet, Nancy Napoli: I am so grateful to each of you for your support and useful feedback throughout the process of this collection!

ABOUT THE AUTHOR

Peggy retired as a Police Lieutenant after 21 years of service with The Village of Tuckahoe Police Department in New York. She is also a graduate of the FBI National Academy, Session 254, in Quantico, Virginia.

Peggy spent most of her career on Patrol as a Supervisor and retired as a Lieutenant in charge of the Juvenile Division and Youth Services. She also taught Law Related Education classes for almost ten years in her local high school and middle school. Peggy is a NYS Police Instructor, and she has been trained and certified in Stress Management. She is currently an independent consultant, providing assessor services, for the New York State Accreditation Program. Today she gives lectures to colleges and groups, and holds workshops on Leadership, Professional Development, Stress Management, and Holistic Wellness.

In 2002, she took her first yoga class and instantly knew that this was the saving grace, a pathway to peace among the daily chaos of life. Her practice gave her the tools to balance raising a family and a demanding career.

She trained at Yoga Haven in New York, and earned her 200-RYT Yoga Instructor certification. She later enrolled in the Institute for Integrative Nutrition in New York City in 2015 and earned her certification as a Health Coach. She studied over one hundred dietary theories, holistic health, the concept of Primary Food (the idea that everything in our life contributes to our inner and outer health), and organic nutrition.

She went on to receive her Kids/Teen Teacher Training certification and is a certified Reiki Practitioner in the Usui Reiki Method of Natural Healing. Peggy's mission was to bring yoga to the community youth and to her brothers and sisters in blue. Today, her scope of practice has expanded to include a large population of senior citizens.

Peggy's passion for writing and poetry has spanned a lifetime, and it led her to become the organizer of the Hudson Writer's Group in New York, which is a community of over 615 writers representing all genres. She has found great joy in supporting other writers and providing a forum for authors to share their work.

In 2015, her belief and passion in a holistic approach to wellness as a means to achieve optimum health, led her to fulfill her desire, and she founded Peggy Belles Transformational Consulting.

Utilizing her wide range of skills and background, she works with clients to improve their health, career and life. She believes the greatest satisfaction lies in helping others realize their fullest potential.

If you are interested in having Peggy speak at your next event, or are interested in any of the services that she offers, please visit her at peggybelles.com, peggybelles.liveeditaurora.com or email her at peggybelles@peggybelles.com

Made in the USA
Middletown, DE
27 September 2023